God's
HEARTBEAT,
POETICALLY EXPRESSED

Heavenly Poet

WESTBOW
PRESS®
A DIVISION OF THOMAS NELSON
& ZONDERVAN

WestBow Press books may be ordered through booksellers or by contacting:

WestBow Press
A Division of Thomas Nelson & Zondervan
1663 Liberty Drive
Bloomington, IN 47403
www.westbowpress.com
844-714-3454

ISBN: 978-1-6642-5955-3 (sc)
ISBN: 978-1-6642-5954-6 (e)

Print information available on the last page.

WestBow Press rev. date: 4/27/2022

Thank you to all who have shown me love and been in support of me

Don't stop loving & living life

Be encouraged & never discouraged just know that Christ is the light

Don't Stop

Like a tree grows, knowledge grows in you. It ignites and takes flight and explodes in you. So don't stop. Don't stop... decree today. Don't stop... declare your way. Because tomorrow is not promised to you anyway. So don't stop! Just start creating, innovating & restoring the people of this world back to their original state. Not just renovating or simulating but rejuvenating ourselves back into God in Christ. For behold all things are made new, all things are made true, all things are made right, made life, made Christ in you. So don't stop. Don't let these knowledge trees and prophecies pass away from you... But yet, let them permeate and trickle-late to make a Life Brand New.

A Poetic Essay...Breaking Generational Curses

I'm pushing pass the pain of my past, I can't allow these problems and life patterns to last. These familiar sin stains are playing like a bad song in my brain, these generational curses are replaying like verses, replaying like verses, I can't rehearse this; I gotta reverse this. How do I progress instead of regress in the residue of shared stains? I wake up, rise up, and realize that Christ reigns. He died and rose again so that we wouldn't have to suffer in guilt and shame, and have our past remain. Speak life and be sustained. The book of life is our food and drink, so let's not get weary and weak, because the adversary can't beat this Daily Bread meant for us to eat. A table has been prepared for the mighty and meek so we won't surrender in defeat, so let us sit down and eat. Regain the energy that family feuds and sleepless nights have since drain, no more crying in the silent nights, get rid of the picture of the pain. It's time out for the blame game, who did what to who and when is sin. Love holds no record of wrongs, only forgives and moves on; no more trash dumps to take home. Gossip feeding our minds and mouths becoming like mold, it gets old. My life's purpose is to kill the cancers contaminating the soul, so I speak life and let love take hold. The power of life and death is in the tongue, so let's speak life so we won't live death by default. These generational curses were caught, some were even taught. From lying to gossip, to different forms of abuse and sexual perversion, these things destroy the foundation of a family if left unchanged. It is sometimes harder to be healed than it is to embrace the pain, because the enemy tricks us to stay enslaved in shame; so don't give way to excuses to remain the same, trade trust for the change. How can we break these familiar chains of bondage, with these family secrets and hidden sins we're in? Stuck in these graves we will remain, if we don't begin to break these fake picture frames. God can't deal with what we refuse to talk about, so walk it out. There's healing in revealing. Wisdom, knowledge, and understanding we gain from comprehending the pain. Let's be reconciled to our brother and clean up the mess we made. Let's take the bands off and stop religiousizing things, using God and the church as a mask to better hide the pain. How can we break these familiar chains of bondage? By recognizing that it's for freedom He came. This poem is about my family, your family, our families being set free from the generational curses that you and I see, so don't stay confused or lost in depression, just be as God intended you to be; truly set free! Because the truth that you know will set you free!

CONTENTS

$\mathcal{A}$ Desolate Place

I heard as I sat in this most desolate place, I am yours and you are Mine, come into My most intimate dwelling place; come in so you don't wither and Seek My Face. Because I am The Tree Of Life and The Vine, and you are My most precious branches so wonderful and divine. Can't you see My love longs for you to be kept wrapped safely in My warm embrace so close to Me? I hear you crying out for Me, continue drawing nearer to Me and Pursue My Peace. As a father lovingly embraces his child, that's how my love calls to thee; I desire you to be as close as you so desperately desire to be. So don't run, duck, and hide in shame from me. I allowed these troubled waters you see, these trials that are still molding you for your destiny. Like an oil press presses olives into oil and a wine press turns grapes into wine, I knew what it would take to shape you and make you look like mine. For these pressures of life are only pruning you for a time, so you can be a shining light; turning wrongs into right before darkness turns into forever night. So don't stop worshipping me, worship only settles you in me. Don't take for granted or despise such small beginnings. Just know that because I've won, you're winning.

Be Content

※

Be content with obscurity because in it lies your security. Be content with not being able to understand everything that you hear and see, because Christ will bring clarity. Wait patiently on the Lord as the overwhelming pressure and pain gets hard to bear, seemingly form to scare, it is reformed to reach and teach the lost; turned into wisdom to help shoulder the crosses we bear. So let us endure our hardship like a good solider, holding steadfast and firm to the promises of The Promise Keeper of The Promise Land. For He who promised is faithful Amen. Don't let the devil cause you to divert from God's plan. Be content to stand because Christ our King is cultivating the land, causing everything to grow and go according to plan. So don't stress on how this race is ran, just be content to stand.

God Is Revealing His Heart

God is revealing His heart for His people, let's get to the heart of matter of these things. It's time for single, married, and family life to be clean. I've seen the condition of our hearts and we're unclean. This poem goes out to the church. This is not a time to shout but a time to selah (stop and calmly think about). God is saddened without a doubt, He chose to use us and not abuse us but we are turning away His love and precious gift of salvation; souring the message He gave us to give to the world and the nations. He gave us an assignment to reach lost, not be the boss. He gave us instructions, simple and certainly not overly exaggerated. Some of us have been doing the absolute most in the Holy Ghost, making His presence a real joke at the most. He said go out and feed my sheep, go out to the uttermost parts of the world; that could mean right up the street. Simply showing our love to our neighbor or helping a friend on their feet, I don't know what it is that has caused many of us to wax cold or conform to the old. He made us to be strong and bold. Walk by faith not sight, be the light in the darkness of the night. I don't know what to say... I'm just a vessel, a garden growing in the kingdom of God just like you, built to build my brothers and sisters up strong and new. These days the wicked are hidden in righteous displays, going to church now it's just fun and games. People are not really being changed. The Lord is tired of our selfish ways. He saved us and changed us to be never the same, to show people that through His love, healing, and miracle working power He reigns. Be transformed and a new life we gain. Don't take this lightly, because it's not the message you thought it might be. These demons are real, and we've been playing games in our Father's harvest field. I can't talk too loud, because I too have sometimes overlooked and lost people in a crowd; distracted by my life to live, I don't have time to save souls and give. we rather Netflix and chill, go to a restaurant, shop and catch this deal. Let's not think about the wounded souls needing to be healed. We got our salvation, so what's the big deal? The big deal is... hell is too hot and eternity is too long to let our souls ride on the devil's Ferris wheel. So, let's get real. Let's be fully committed to this life with Christ and make sure our hearts are never Satan's to steal. Some people can be in church a good 50 years and never really seal the deal. So, let's do it right in His sight and stand 4real, putting on garments of salvation and a robe of righteousness makes it eternally real.

I Am My Brother's Keeper

I am my brother's keeper that's why I push pass my past to carry the burden of freedom, because I know your heart really bleeds for us your people. I worship you with my tears to show you how much I appreciate and need you, don't make the rocks cry out, they don't need to. I cling to Your Word that transforms me like a bird; an eagle that soars like The Living Word that I heard. There's no more church with a door and a steeple, more like the temple of the living God in Christ birthed in the bodies of Your people. I shout out to the ones that ain't saved, don't be afraid to join us; these former sin slaves. I cry out until I die out, I love you! Don't wait and hope to go to heaven to be saved, He paid the price for all of us and its beautiful on the other of the side of the grave. The world has created such delightful delusions and deceptions to keep you oppressed and in chains. It is Satan's sweet delight to keep you blind to his games. Some people might say I come off too rich, too churchy or too spiritual for some ears to make sense; but when it comes to Christ, His riches are worth it. I can't water down the Word because there's too much truth in it to gain. He came to change the game and make our lives never the same. So don't sleep, you need the living water and the meat to get out the chains. They hollin stay woke. I'm hollin stay awake and alive in Christ, be aware of the tricks and games. Don't feed into the high philosophes of those who have sold their souls for their names. The you that you know is only a fragment of your true self, your new self is hidden in The One who was slain. I dare you to trust Him and let your lives be changed. His love is off the chain and you'll be surprise to see what comes out of living a true kingdom lifestyle. He reigns

Hooked On Phonics For Ebonics

When I first learned about Ebonics I thought it was a fad that was fading fast, a trendy idiom that wasn't going to last. When I reluctantly adapted to it, I discovered that this language had been around a lot longer than I had. From Fred Astaire and Duke Ellington being cool hip cats teaching us how to tap jive and swing. And Good Times touch on how to enjoy life when the struggle gets too real, JJ keeping it Dynomite and James and Florida Evans teaching us how to let LOVE heal. The Jeffersons who moved on up to the eastside while staying down to earth and hip to what was happening in their hometown. These famous celebrities and this fictional families helped bring Ebonics to the forefront of today's many languages. Ebonics transcended time evolving through TV media and music into a cool way of communicating. It added flava to some people's otherwise dry and dreary personalities. When hip-hop hit the scene, it was like everyone became hooked-on phonics for Ebonics; bringing a fun and positive message to things. It went from being a creative way of speaking using less words and syllables, but still somewhat sensible, to completely silly and senseless. Where are the rhythms of grace that were so ingrained in our character and our part of speech? As was displayed in The Cosby Show as they taught us a sense of class and family values while chillaxin in the living room. What is the lesson that we teach? That it's cool to be a fool? Naw not at all. Even the hiphop pioneers had an element of eloquence and education, as they spat their dope lines and made us reflected on our everyday lives. Using the universal language of Ebonics, hiphop artists dealt with issues ranging from drug abuse to social change. But lately I've been feeling a spirit of frustration or maybe it is God's righteous indignation, rising up in me, because this now hiphop-idiocrisy that some our presenting has seemingly singly corrupted the nation; bringing with it a behavioral infestation. Turning what was once a powerful craft into trash not to be admired, destroying our characters, and it's a rap going into the fire. That's why we are lost in translation, having convulsions of insanity, transforming all humanity.

Jesus Is Hope

Jesus is hope when you're going down a slope. His Word an antidote for an addict to cope. No need to smoke. Let His Word put you in a heavenly haze. Don't give your mind to swine. The Word helps the drug user and drug dealer not just to endure, but to cling to life; and remember there's hope at the end of the rope. Hold onto God's grace, don't disqualify yourself in the race. Know that because of His love you are not replaced. You were not put here to see your life end early, but to win. Put your ear to the gentle voice in the wind. Your relationship with The Living God matters, don't lose your hope trying to climb the latter. Workaholics exists leaving their lives amiss. An Alcoholics life creates all types of shenanigans, painting you as a clown; But you must get drunk in the spirit in save your life now. Don't get lost in such evil wayz, allowing the devil to put in a daze. He does these negative things, to keep you curled up so cold in a cave; until you find yourself in an early grave. When you attempt to change your ways and you find yourself in the presence of the living God, worshipping His holy name, reminded that Jesus saves; let the holy ghost and fire set the drama and mess ablaze. Get lost in the heavenlies where your new life begins in a wave.

Once Upon A Time

Once a upon a time in a world that now seems so far away, we lived in a considerably peaceful environment. What ever happened to those good old days where little kids could go outside and play, be safe, stay on the sidewalk and don't talk to strangers is what their parents would say. Because neighborhood watchers would be watching the streets, helping to keep the peace, assisting the police. It's no longer a beautiful day in the neighborhood, somebody save the hood, these things have changed for good. Somebody said it takes a village to raise a child, but where is that village now? While the people of this village are catnapping, the children are becoming lost. Being killed or kidnapped or sold away, let's pray and LOVE will heal our broken hearts so don't stray. What's really going on? The children are growing up on their own; losing their identity not to mention their virginity. Some kids are rioting and setting themselves on fire, while the grandparents and parents play let's be young again today, being blinded to their children's pain and dismay. What has caused this drastic change in our minds hearts and lives? Because the fear of God is gone from the land and no one is content to stand.

Once Upon A Time Two

Once upon a time we lived in a land where in God we trust was more than a motto, it was our declaration and decree upon which we followed. Now the hearts of the people are hollow. Where is the love of God that was shown in our stride, His peace that marked our hearts and transformed lives? These boys and girls are confused in this world; with their self-worth, self-esteem, and self-image being tainted and lost in a swirl. They can't see straight the way for these hell stones twist and curves that have led them astray; for this is the path of those who love the world; their footsteps being led by a prince and a curse, preparing them for hell. The enemy is rising in pride, the people are spiritually dying inside. Where are the ones the living God has chosen to lead the lost, the righteous who He gave the power to stand? Where are those who are supposed to abide in His love, show His mercy and grace, and lead the lost of this land to His dwelling place? The godly need to help the godless. Why all this injustice, evil, and wickedness? Because the righteous aren't answering the call of command, we need some living stones to breathe life in these dry bones; speak life into the lukewarm and the cold. The Lord of the harvest is soon to arrive, so don't sleep or slumber it's time to arise. This may be one of the last calls for the righteous to stand tall, be bold and courageous or you may fall.

1 Peter 2:4-9 NKJV NLT MSG

We Must Not Muzzle Our Mouths

We must not put a muzzle on our mouths, it's a time to be quiet and a time to speak out, there's a sort of righteous indignation we need to have to change the nation. In other words, get gangsta on the devil to be heard, we fight not against flesh and blood so don't misunderstand these words. Like when he had a sword in his mouth and fire in his eyes, he didn't come to bring peace; but the truth of his word and a holy divide. We can't stay stuck between two worlds. We must stay on a mission, and that mission dies in the valley of decision. Like oil and water can't mix, light and darkness together just doesn't make sense. Jesus came to embrace the brokenhearted and clean up the dirty, he didn't come to compromise but open blinded eyes. Don't be surprise when you see His children rise, transform and ascend to heaven right before your eyes! But some will say, aren't we all God's children tho? Inquiring minds wanna know. We are all God's creation, but it takes a true confession of your belief in Christ to go. We can't transform ourselves and expect the evidence to show. Do not conform to the ways this world, but be transform by the renewing of our minds through His Word; to be wise in our own eyes is a crime and it only works to fast-forward our demise. We must expose these wolves in sheep clothing, take note of the seasons and times. God is speaking to the young and old, don't get trapped in the game you were sold. We gotta turn up in Christ and tune in to the spirit behind the beat leading us into deceit, sin shaped in different forms of Godliness is foolishness at its finest. On one side we are saying come from among them and be set apart, and on the other side we are saying we must do like Jesus did. Jesus ate lunch with the sinners and His love lead them out of sin. There's no compromising

17

in holiness, but where is the middle ground in all of this? The place where the righteous and the runner meet, mercy and loving kindness kiss when they greet, and we give grace to the sinner to finally see. We must listen to The Spirit of God and He'll lead us to do what's best indeed.

2 Corinthians 6:14 Romans 10:9 Romans 12:2 Proverbs 3:7 Mark 2:13-17 Psalm 85:10

What Is The Color Of Love

Oh my, the dead has arisen! The Ku Klux Klan and these racist groups and fans have all come out and they are back on commission; this devil's on a mission. We really need to unite in Christ and seek the Father's guidance day and night. These senseless killings just isn't right. You need to pick up the sword of the Spirit instead of your gun and your knife, God's Word and wisdom guides you to do what's right. Tell me what color is Christ? He lost His life and shed His blood pure red to save your life. Replace that gun in your hand for His weapons of warfare and shout for His Glory to return. His Kingdom is at hand. He weeps at every dead body in these streets. For He is the color of love sent from above and there is no place for hate in His Holy Place. For He loves every color of the human race, and your actions have just been a spit in His face. It's time to repent and show a little mercy and grace. He loves even the darkest of those blinded by religious cults and those whose minds are completely lost. But you can be reconcile to God and through your life He will teach, the broken hearts of this nation how His forgiveness will come to fruition and it will be a transforming life lesson.

You Can't Gag, Order or
Body Bag This Mouth

———— ⚜ ————

You can't gag or order or bodybag this mouth, my tongue was created and poised to shout! The Lord maketh not ashamed, so if you're hiding come out. For perfect love cast out all fear and doubt. The blood in these streets are crying speak my name and stop this senseless killing game; for the innocent souls we lost are heaven's gain. The Lord rules and reigns, He's out for justice and to heal the pain. Vengeance is mine said the Lord, so don't try to be a vigilante and die in vain. You'll only be adding to the people's pain. Don't let gun violence and racial division remain; for these reoccurring missiles are on a self-destructing mission to kill and destroy God's vision. These stereotypes and racial prejudices were seen when Dr. Martin Luther King had a dream, so don't let our people repeat the same thing. But let's reconstruct to form CHRIST The KING'S Dream, and be an actual representation of what one nation under God really means. Much love and respect to those who love ones have endure suffering, and even lost their lives due to gun violence. So remember black lives as well as all lives really do matter. Peace and many prayers for you.

Understanding God

From the gun shots, to the earthquakes and the whirlwinds of sickness and disease, people say where is God in mist of this? Some say these things are happening because people fail to seek You, while that may be true, forgive us for being insensitive and not knowing how to lead people to You. Because what about the people who were never taught how to seek You? Let us be reminded of how to gently lead people to Jesus Christ as Your holy word instructs us to do.

The struggling working mother with four kids needs to know that You make all things new but not through a religion but a true relationship with You. Help me understand You anew; because this old-time religion and tradition are leading people away from You. You are a healer and deliverer, but Your people have to let You shine through. God, I ask you to let the real and righteous rise up, and restore people's hopes and dreams in You. Let's not condemn people because they know not what they do, help them to stand strong and let's stand together to show that faith expresses itself through love. That's how we acknowledge The One from above.

Luke 23:34 Galatians 5:6 6:1

Where is our Faith

What can we say to these matters that will ease our minds and heal our human race? Where are those who are found in God's grace? Where is our faith the size of a mustard seed that can move mountains as we believe? Where is our faith? To be knocked down but not out To be bent but not broken, how we are supposed to be prayer and worship warriors, we have to get to the point of having the mind of Christ. Creating an atmosphere of faith so that we don't lose heart in this state. The bible says that we are ought to be a light as Christ is and be a light that brings revelation to the gentiles, the unbelievers need Jesus Christ now. As Christians suffer, they are not ashamed. we must have faith to move beyond the fight, so let us remember the pain and anguish not another night.

Roman 8:31 Matthew 17:20 Luke 2:32 1 Peter 4:16

What's Going On With Us?

What is going on with US? The people of the USA? That our country is starting not to belong to us. First it was the racist rants shootings and killings, taking the lives of people we can't ever get back. Now people are storming the US Capitol like they're dummies, I'm so sick of this childish nonsense, it ain't even funny. Where are the adults who are supposed to be leaders running the country? So much is handled without any intelligence or tact, leaving a lot of our future leaders to grow up ill-trained, untamed, presenting themselves as inferior, and just lame, without any sense of proper instruction or direction to claim. No one but ignorance to blame. The great history of those who blazed the trail before us seemingly put to shame; we can't even function the same. It's so devastating to see our country in so much pain, the people are left racking their brains to push through the pain of a pandemic leaving us to plead Jesus name. So many hearts may be failing in faith, but Psalms 91:10 says: No plague shall come near my dwelling just be healed, for the power of Christ Jesus is real. So just know that if you believe, by Jesus stripes your healed. The question is how do we get back to focus? I believe if we trace the tracks of the trailblazers such as: Martin Luther King Jr, John Lewis, Oral Roberts, Former President Barack Obama, and T.D. Jakes that went ahead of us, we will be encouraged to be bold; to let the purpose of our lives take shape and be sustained when we're old. But we must return to The Word and try to forget what we've seen and heard. With everything becoming so black and white, we must seek Christ and let our character be restored by God's grace. Jesus desires for us to experience His love, His joy and perfect peace while we wait for change to take place. Let's pray for The President & those in authority, letting His Presence be our comforting place. This poem is dedicated to President Biden and VP Kamala Harris. Thank you for example! You are among the greatest of trailblazers!

Romans 13 Acts 4:30 Matthew 14:14

Miracle Worker

I am seeing the miracle worker work miracles that are seemly unreal, physically and spiritually mind blown; as myself and others lives are being transformed and healed. It's like being knocked out by the heaviest of heavyweights, as the Holy Spirit fills us and reveals to us God's power through His grace. We tread upon the wicked in this new and improved state. Religion has had us looking for a sign, a onetime miraculous experience to take place. But the miracle is in our lives changing daily as we enter into His grace, this wonderful resting place. Streams of living water flowing causing His purposes to take shape. We receive freedom from all forms of bondage, as we are saved and safe. I'm a sponge as I soak in this living water that was spoken. Seeing us exhale this pain and strife and inhale The Breath Of Life, I'm amazed by this marvelous sight. I love to live in His dwelling place day and night, where miracles are God made for the supernatural; not man made for the spectacular. Man can't conceive or contrive the power of the miraculous; only The Miracle Worker can manifest this.

Water

Refreshing like a cool breeze blowing cold through the trees.

As it is sprinkled on your face, the action of this feeling like amazing grace

Better than your best day what more can I say?

Streams of living water flowing

Serene pure tranquility so supreme

The taste of it, droplets sliding down your tongue to your spine, sending shockwaves through your body alerting you that your alive! Water is healthy to revitalize your mind. Wake up it's time! Like a waterfall signaling to a rainbow a new day is mine. Experiencing the creation of water is truly sublime!

A Creative Mind

A creative mind is unlocked through time

Traveling in slow motion, absorbing all artistic & poetic expression

A good inspirational poem is written and expressed by words from the heart. To inspire, encourage, and motivate mankind. It tells a story, paints a picture, and brings life to the body and soul. A key connected to The Creator of all creation and is simply divine. Growth, stimulating and necessary to teach, heal, and shape the nation.

We Are Leaders

<hr />

We are leaders who are being led as we lead. We are prophets and prophetesses who are always being prophesied to, and we are evangelists who are always being evangelized. We are preachers who are told what to preach and teachers who are still being taught as we teach. But who are we first? Are we just a product of the five fold ministry? or are we children of God, who are formed in His image and likeness, who are still being trained in the ways of The Way. Are we self-manifested or are we a creation created by The Creator to create? Do we actually need to put on our apostolic ears to hear God say: come to me my child? I love you, come walk and talk with me. For it is true that the Deep calls to the deep, but He is not always calling to reveal this grand plan. A good leader is one who listens and understands that he or she is first and foremost a child in the Father's hands.

The lost generation

I am a part of a very peculiar society of people, the last of what seems to be a dying breed. Many of the elders of this society grew up in the backwoods and countryside of America, and they were taught some ancient customs and a foreign language; in which they passed down from generation to generation. These almost extinct customs and unique language, although strange and irrelevant today, helped shape the core morals and values of this US of A. What exactly am I referring to? The foundation of good manners and the holy language called prayer. Since when is it repulsive to be polite? I am an alien being alienated by my own peers because I remember how to be respectful, in the words of my generation: where they do that at? To speak with intelligence and to say yes ma'am or no ma'am is completely castaway. Yes, the times have extremely changed, but does the core of our country have to change as well? It is argued that this generation and the next are The lost generations, but who or what is truly lost? That is to be determined.

True Parental Guidance

When do I get to be over 21? My ID no longer stating under 21 signifies that maturity has transpired and a level of responsibility is required. Honor your mother and father is ingrained in us to do to the best of our ability. You as parents, so overbearing and domineering, that you begin overprotecting who is already protected. Because in His tough yet unconditional love, He still takes good care of His child. But He doesn't spare the rod. The relationship between parents and children should be evident. Not appearing as a picture, but real connection of a mother and daughter father and son, a true bond that is meant to be shared or vice versa. Because a daughter needs her daddy among other things, and a mother is meant teach her son how to care. A parent should celebrate their child's accomplishments, instead provoking them to anger and stopping their shine. But no, what the parent says goes. It's my way or the highway, that is forever made known. Forget the instructions you as a parent are to uphold. You can make your children so actively inactive, sociably disabled preparing them for a living grave; while being parentally enslaved. Provoking them to abort God's ways. You gotta give them room to walk the path that was paved, watch out that you don't unknowingly provoke them to be disobedient or misbehave. It is the unconditional love of Christ and The Father's loving discipline I recommend. To bring out the best in them so that their hearts will mend to win.

The Road Of Spiritual And Physical Suicide

I was thinking about how many go down the road of spiritual and physical suicide, trippin out on the negative thoughts flowing in their heads causing double mindedness and spiritual or physical deathbed. Denying Jesus Christ destroys your life, and it is to hell you are lead. You gotta listen what Jesus is saying keeping you Spirit lead, don't let images of darkness dance in your head. Don't let negative words turn into murder weapons, killing you and others when they're said. You must breathe in The Word of God, and stop marrying demons, waking up in cold sweats in bed. Stop letting delusions fill your minds, forming depression in the disguise. He said just know that I am and I will always be there. Don't let the devil ride, just know that Christ cares and He will see you to the other side of life's rollercoaster ride.

Proverbs 12:18 Proverbs 15:4 John 8:12 Matthew 28:20 1 Peter 5:7

God Said I Love You Still

God said I love you still. I love you with an everlasting love. Even though you are running away from me, I have not left you or forsaken you. Even though you are disobeying Me, I am forever faithful. Even though you are not acknowledging me, I know you have not forgotten Me or my word. Because I have placed conviction in you, I know you will come back to Me. Just has a child who disobeys his or her mother or father and runs away, so have you done. Nevertheless, when that child recognizes they're wrong, he or she comes running back. That's why I am never worried, for your conviction will always return you to Me. This is only for my children. Those who have never known Me as their God, Father, or Jesus as their Savior and made aware of their sins can never feel convicted.

We Must Not Contaminate Ourselves

See we are special, like the first pair of Air Jordans or like a fine wine to The Divine something to treasure. We must not allow ourselves to be contaminated by the weed, pill poppin or the bump n grind; only allowing our process in life to be perverted over time. But let us be secure in the blood of Jesus The Divine. He holds our secrets and gently keeps us in line; always letting us know that He got us, keeps us on our grind and always ready to shine. Don't underestimate this Spirit-to-spirit vibe, it's the real thing, a true love worth it to find. The purity, security and sacredness, a real connection to Jesus will keep us on our feet. Jesus being God's son is the best thing and no one can compete, because He opens us up to the fact that we're his children too and stunnin like our Daddy is the best thing that we could ever do. The Holy Spirit is able to comfort us when we going through the realest struggle we ever knew. Staying on point with Him is more than just a hook up, preparing you for that true friend, husband or wife in due time. The good about this relationship from us to eternity back into time is incredibly hard for us to find. To compare it to anything on earth would be holy matrimony between a man and woman, a true tie that binds. That's why I contemplate being married to the trinity only, staying single and not necessarily to mingle; but to be whole in me though. But let God's Will be done not mine. The adversary knows how to spiritually bind, that's why we must keep to the Cross and allow God to answer our questions over time. Because He knows best and His Kingdom is meant to be eternally yours and mine. This poem is about keepin it real with God and maintaining that forever vibe. Because heaven is where home is. Stay Real, Rise n Shine.

Matthew 9:17 Romans 10:9 2 Corinthians 5:17 John 14:16-17 26. NKJV NLT MSG

Found Home

Let the devil and all the demons in hell scream and holler and hate and all of heaven rejoice. Because a lost soul has now found their way, because a lost soul who was lost yesterday is now found today. She's found her way home in Your presence, home with your people, she's found her way home to truth and she's found her way home to You. Let the dead in sin be borne again, broken to mend; let the healing begin. She has, he has, they have, and we all have found our home anew.

The Experience: How To Weather Any Weather

❧

I'm up just talking to The Father about this experience I've been having, unlike anything I'm used to having. it's as if I'm under these demonic forces, under some demonic attack that doesn't seem to cease; disturbing my peace. But strangely I've stayed rooted and grounded in God's presence, not surrendering to defeat as Immanuel counsels the direction of my feet; I remember it's God's Word that causes me to see. Whatever the situation tries to bring, even causing an odd disconnected; but I'm not put to shame. The disconnect occurs when I'm just focused on these things. I've been walking with the Trinity for awhile now, and I refuse to bow down to the devil's tactics and at times comical theatrics. Because he's been out to make me weak and cause confusion so I can't sleep. I've been walking in the Spirit since 2008 receiving the evidence of speaking in tongues, how sweet to taste. The devil keeps existing to hate. As I've learned about The Father, The Son, and The Holy Spirit every day in every way, sometimes I've experienced such a warped experience; where everything that isn't God is manifesting around me, trying to overtake and crowd me. Such as senseless arguments that have led to nowhere, and manifestations of the devil tryna punk me and cause me to abort God's Will. That's why it's very crucial that we take our relationship with God serious and the fact that He exist point blank period. We have so many people who believe in Jesus, and many that don't believe us. If the only bible that people read is us "believers" as we say we believe in The King, then how can they overcome these things? If we fail to fight in the ring? These battles in life called spiritual warfare that the devil brings? Being in example of why Christ is The King. The Heavenly Father's army always outnumbers the devil's. That's why it's important that we stay transitioning with His Word, so we won't self-destruct and utterly fail, our destination leading to hell. Can't you tell as these roads begin to curve twisting our minds and emotions as they swerve? Don't fall asleep on these devilish attacks that are harmful to you that only Jesus can help you beat. For example, those battling with mental disorders, those in LGBTQ community who many battle with their identity and being accepted and wonder why? It's because The Creator created them to fit in His divine design, but it's only the enemy tryna cause them to unravel and make them lose their minds. Don't settle for spending our lives battling with the devil, but let's use the weapons that God The Creator of heaven and earth and everything in them gives us to win in any weather, and let's know that it will get better when we believe we can weather any weather.

Don't Be A Slave Or Slain

Don't be a slave or slain, working a 9 to 5 to put food on the table and stay sane. The Word says your gift will make room for you, so let's work on discovering ourselves anew. Let's not pour our lives into what doesn't breathe life into us. We were meant to be lit, not play a puppet in this world's puppeteer games. let God establish your name. Show them you are not a slave to the mentalities and stereotypes of this world, let earth see God through your eyes. Don't live life suffering living in despise and despair. Don't stay under 21, too immature and green to understand what life really means. If you have understanding, walk it out, don't just talk it out. Live it loud and shout it stand out.

Remember to thank the Lord

No matter what, we must always remember to have something to thank God for & to praise God for. The Holy Spirit is the key to perfect peace in life & total victory as we are reminded of the voice of Christ Jesus. Everything we have don't belong to us, we're just getting the use of it. Everything we have God gave us, so just praise Him & know that church is in your heart first.

Don't Lack Knowledge

The Word says that our people are destroyed for lack of knowledge and let's not forget we've been blessed with common sense. So why are we reacting like this? This is not the time or the hour to act like cowards but raise our voice in power. Speak life over the situations every hour. Some of us our constantly living in the negative, feeling like we're dying with this pandemic leaving us crying. We gotta start speaking hope to our dreams and be refueled by King. Speak joy comes in the morning. Let not your hope be deferred when a new day is dawning. Let Christ Jesus breathe new life over these sick and deathbeds in faith and truth. Let our sanity be restored giving us a clear conscious and clarity as our anchor board. God preserves our youth, keeps us revitalized and strengthen anew. I'm not just speaking to those who already gave their lives to Christ, I'm speaking to the lost souls just tryna survive. The Word tells us about a Savior who gave us everlasting life. It's time to think right, not let our souls continue to become corrupted and bodies turn old. Where sin abides, grace much more abides. We gotta stay thinking about The Light to bounce back right and know that our hope is only found in Christ. Be loud when you're shutting the devil down. Don't be a punk just stuck in the crowd. The struggle is real. Jesus knows how we feel. We gotta ride out of our difficulties on faith while we seek God's face.

We've Come Through

We've come through some challenging and very difficult times. Through fears and so many tears, almost losing our minds. We've gotta remember there's hope. As we say, we've gotta mountain to climb. But, how about asking God to remove the mountain?

As you meditate, just let The Word marinate. Meditating on anything but Jesus, these days, is a crime. Why do I say that? Because the enemy comes to steal, kill, and destroy our body and mind at all times. We've been through so much, it's been hard to keep in touch with reality sometimes. But, it's the plot and plan of the devil tho, to get us outta focus... hocus pocus. What we've been through is far from fun and games, It has been a challenge just to maintain. From The Black Lives Matters Movement, to the pandemic; we need reminders of The Light, who is life to restore healing again.

When you were enslaved, He broke the chains so that you can enjoy much better days. He came to give life. So, remember that there's no grave.

The Woman In The Mirror

What does the woman in the mirror see? Is her beauty only skin deep or does she see beyond her complexion and countenance, straight through to her heart, soul, and spirit? Does she see the many unhealed wounds and scares from her, still haunting, past? Or does she envision her fulfilled future? A revelation of her, soon to be, reality; as her rivers and streams of hurt and pain unfold, she is suddenly, revived as she floats into real life. An ocean, full of beautifully, uncharted waters, awaiting to be discovered, intricately woven pools of pure love and purpose that are, divinely, designed by her tears. Who is this woman in the mirror? A beautiful dream, yet unseen.

The Complexities Of A Sophisticated Lady

A woman is not defined by her beauty, shape or size but rather an inner divine design. Her lovely twists and curves lie in the extremities of her mind in which no man can unwind. She is edgy, yet elegant; earthly, yet extremely intelligent. Her timid voice speaks volumes and her quiet beauty captures the hearts of many men. She does not consist of the things she possesses. Her existence is not materialized. Can she not dwell among the rich because she does not wear the latest fashion designs or drink the finest wine? Is she not considered worthy enough to converse with the intellectuals because she speaks with a throwback ghetto vernacular? Does her unique and diverse language speak of her intelligence, or does it suggest that she can relate to the unrelatable? Who can judge? Man or God? For these are the complexities of a sophisticated lady.

He Put Me Together

⸻❦⸻

He put me together in His love He made me better, told me how to move on through stormy weather. He said: Have faith and hold tight til I make it right, I will see you through this fight. Beloved I can see you in the tender light, don't run from God's gentle love taps, it will be alright. I made you more than a conqueror, don't be scared to fight. Don't suppress your depression not another night. Open your heart and let me fill your cup once more, you ache because you closed the door. I miss holding you in my warm embrace, you got confused because you let someone else take my place. True enough I sent someone to run with you in this race, but be patient you're not even halfway to the gate. Christ love holds on true love will wait, stay tuned and remember to work while you wait. Don't rush; I'm putting my Kingdom into place. I will set the time and the date.

Jesus Keep Me

Jesus keep me near the cross as I travel down this lonely road of lust vs love, which one do I hold. Preparing for marriage and actually being married is not for the weak, you must stay strong and ask God to take hold. True love God's love is worth waiting for. Don't waste your time giving your body, emotions, and mind away to what's not divine, hold on to the vine. Jesus is that precious wine. He makes love last and kills the physical, mental and emotional strongholds of the past. Sometimes He has to break what we think is love for us to take hold of His holy hand and remember His plan. Because whether we be man or woman, He's still our husband. But it's not about being married or given in marriage, it's about advancing the kingdom. So be wise before you say I do and make spiritual soul ties that bind both your bodies and your lives, we must stay behind the veil before the time to awaken love arrives.

Break Out Of The Chains

Break out the chains of long ago slavery days, of always following a master's ways instead of going The Master's Way. Break out of the chains that bind you, break out of the chains that do not define you, break out of the chains of utter destruction and death. Those long ago slavery days of whips and chains are no more, but this world seems to be stuck in yesterday's miseries; too blinded by the prince of darkness to realize that they've been set free. They're too busy playing puppets and puppeteers for the plantation masters of today. So, come out those invisible chains and stop being mentally enslaved, because The Chain-Breaker has broken the chains, The WayMaker has already made a way, and The Master of Freedom has already come to save the day.

No Longer Carrying The Weights

No longer carrying the weights, No Longer weighed down by endless struggles and life's dramatic displays. Oh what a path to take as I entered the heavenly gates, why must people wait. As life unwinds and we go through space and time we enter our Savior's embrace. Thank God for his mercy and grace. The golden streets of heaven awaits, mansions made of marble what a glorious sight come and stay. But the real gift is what The King Of Glory will say, after you have told His story and seen his mercy and grace: Well done my good faithful servant, come in and sit down your heavenly home awaits.